IRON VIOLIN PUBLISHERS

GIFTS

VENUE

WEDDING CAKE

Mike
&
Elsa

LIMOUSINE

PEWCHAIR BOWS

You & Me
TOGETHER FOREVER

CANDLES

SHOES

MANICURE

LIMOUSINE

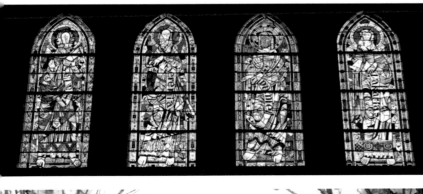

FROM THIS DAY Forward

FLOWER PETALS

FIRST DANCE

GARTER

BRIDESMAIDS

Bride squad

MANICURE

GROOMSMEN

FOOD

FLOWER GIRLS

PHOTOGRAPHER

CHAMPAGNE

VENUE

ATTIRE

Our love Story

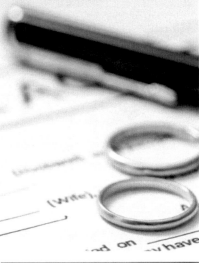

TUXEDO

Our ♥ moment

VENUE

JUST MARRIED

we are better together

GUESTBOOK

LIGHTING

NTERTAINMENT

HONEYMOON

Our ♥ moment

BRIDAL GOWN

GIFTS

VIP CLUB

SHOES

I love you
I love you
I love you
I love you

WEDDING CAKE

LIQUOR

LIMOUSINE

BRIDESMAIDS

INVITATION

FLOWERS

BRIDAL GOWN

WEDDING CAKE

FAVORS

CANAPES

WEDDING VOWS

MAKEUP

TABLE SETTINGS

BOUQUET

RINGS

TABLE SETTINGS

FOOD

SPA

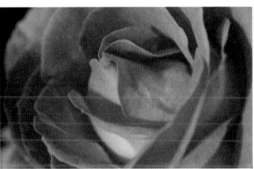

HONEYMOON

VENUE

HOTEL

WEDDING CAKE

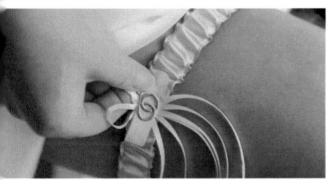

VINTAGE

CHAIR SASHES

DECORATIONS

STATIONARY

FLOWERS

FIRST DANCE

CEREMONY

Save the Date

MUSIC

BOUTONNIERE

with love... from

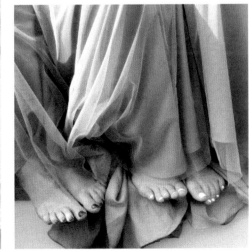

BRIDAL GOWN

BOUQUET

JEWELRY

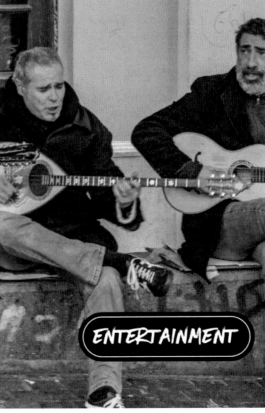

ENTERTAINMENT

for that most
wonderful day...

...nning a wedding can be fun—and
...t in the field of weddin...
...urself. This...

Wedding Day

GUESTBOOK

PHOTOGRAPHY

HONEYMOON

ROSE PETALS

DIRECTIONS

EXIT

Made in the USA
Las Vegas, NV
16 November 2024

11943338R00052